LIVSWEET
OLIVIA ROSENFELD

PHOTOGRAPHS BY
OLIVIA ROSENFELD
AND SOPHIE MAIN

FIRST EDITION

Edited and designed by Beth Bracken
Photograph on back cover by Jackie Schellbach

ISBN: 978-0-9600375-0-6

To Mom, Dad, and Beth
Thank you for all the help along the way.

TABLE OF CONTENTS

INTRODUCINGOLIVIA

Hello!

My name is Olivia Rosenfeld. I live in New York City with my parents and my dogs, and I've been baking for basically my entire life. I was drawn to baking as a kid and started out with box mixes. Soon I decided that I wanted to make more things from scratch, so I started using different cookbooks and online recipes, learning more and more each time I made something new.

My love of baking started at a young age.

In 7th grade, I was baking almost every weekend and I was beginning to develop a real understanding of how ingredients work together and what tastes I really liked. My mom's friend knew how much I enjoyed baking – and that I did it well. She asked if she could hire me to bake cupcakes for a luncheon she was having. Of course I said yes, and that was the beginning of my business...kind of.

Starting a business at age 13 takes a lot of coordination, and it took me a while to get the hang of it. Like all kids my age, I had a lot on my plate: homework, sports, friends, family time, etc., and having a baking business on top of that meant putting aside the time and the energy to make it work. A heart-to-heart conversation with my grandmother over my winter break in 2016 motivated me to get serious about the business, and that's when Olivia Luv Bake Shop became real to me. I started baking more and more, building a customer base, speaking about the business, and developing recipes. But I made mistakes along the way! At first I ordered way too much expensive edible glitter – I wouldn't recommend this to new entrepreneurs, but I was so excited to make my treats the most extravagant on the market.

Something I knew when I started my business was that I wanted to give back to my community, so I donate 20% of my profits each year to organizations like the ASPCA, Memorial Sloan Kettering Cancer Center and the ALS Association. All of these resonate with me very personally and I want to support them in any way I can.

I hope you will enjoy making and sharing my recipes!

Olivia

Me and my friend, Navah, selling cupcakes to vice-presidential candidate Senator Tim Kaine; my Olivia Luv Bake Shop logo.

BEFOREYOUBEGIN

Here are some general notes and tips to help make the most out of my recipes.

1. Because everyone's oven is different, if anything looks raw or undercooked after the instructed time, leave in the oven; checking in 2-3 minute increments should do the trick.

2. To "whip" butter, place your butter (and your other ingredients if instructed) into a standing electric mixer on high speed for about 20 seconds; if you are using an electric hand mixer, mix on high speed for 2 minutes. If by hand, rigorously stir until you achieve a light, creamy texture.

3. Whenever you use eggs in a recipe, always crack them in a separate bowl so that you can remove any excess shell before adding the eggs to the batter or dough.

4. If your frosting ever seems too runny, don't give up! You can slowly but surely add small amounts of confectioners sugar into your mixture until it has reached the consistency that you would like.

5. I always spray cooking spray on my cupcake pans before I put the liners in and fill them. In case the cupcakes spill over while in the oven, this helps you take them out of the pan without the liner getting stuck and ripping.

6. On the next few pages you'll find my favorite tools that I find make baking sweeter and more fun.

FAVORITE TOOLS

The kitchen tools that I use the most help bring
out the best in all my recipes.

My pink stand mixer is essential for consistency
and speed – and I love how it looks.

FAVORITE TOOLS

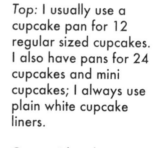

Top: I usually use a cupcake pan for 12 regular sized cupcakes. I also have pans for 24 cupcakes and mini cupcakes; I always use plain white cupcake liners.

Center: I lay down parchment paper for all cookie and many treat recipes. It comes in a roll and I cut it with scissors to fit my pan; the pan shown is a sheet pan. I use it for cookies and bars.

Bottom: This is my one-dozen donut pan. I have loved creating recipes for this.

FAVORITE TOOLS

A trusty plastic spatula is a must.

I keep a variety of colors, shapes and sizes of sprinkles together in a drawer.

I keep all my piping tools together in a portable organizer box.

CUPCAKES

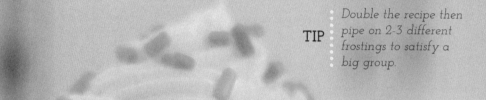

TIP *Double the recipe then pipe on 2-3 different frostings to satisfy a big group.*

This is currently my most popular cupcake, but when first developing the recipe, I had trouble getting the cupcakes to rise. I tried a bunch of combinations of baking soda and baking powder, regular sugar and light brown sugar. I finally got the taste I love but they were still a little flat. Then I realized it just makes them perfect for piping on lots of frosting!

VANILLACUPCAKES

Makes 12 cupcakes

INGREDIENTS

- ¾ cup softened unsalted butter
- ½ cup sugar
- ½ cup packed light brown sugar
- 2 eggs
- 1 cup flour
- 1 ¼ teaspoons baking powder
- ¼ teaspoon salt
- ¼ cup whole milk
- 1 teaspoon vanilla extract

DIRECTIONS

1. Preheat the oven to 350°F.
2. Whip the butter until fluffy.
3. Add both sugars.
4. Crack eggs into a small, separate bowl then add them to the butter/sugar mixture.
5. Combine the flour, baking powder, and salt (the dry ingredients) in a separate bowl.
6. Combine the milk and vanilla extract (the wet ingredients) in a measuring cup.
7. Alternate adding the wet and dry ingredients into the butter mixture until fully combined.
8. Lightly grease a cupcake pan and put in liners; fill ½ - ¾ of each liner with batter.
9. Bake cupcakes for 8 minutes, rotate the pan, and bake for another 9 minutes.

SUGGESTED FROSTINGS

There is nothing more perfectly decadent than a chocolate cupcake topped with chocolate or caramel frosting! My recipe is super chocolatey, rich, and delicious, and goes best with a glass of milk.

CHOCOLATE CUPCAKES

Makes 12 cupcakes

INGREDIENTS

- ¾ cup softened unsalted butter
- 1 cup sugar
- ½ cup packed light brown sugar
- 1 egg
- 1 cup all purpose flour
- 1 ¼ teaspoons baking powder
- ¼ teaspoon salt
- 1 cup cocoa powder
- ½ cup whole milk
- 1 teaspoon vanilla extract

DIRECTIONS

1. Preheat the oven to 350°F.
2. Whip the butter until fluffy.
3. Add both sugars.
4. Crack the egg into a small, separate bowl then add it to the butter/sugar mixture.
5. Combine the flour, baking powder, salt, and cocoa powder (the dry ingredients) in a separate bowl.
6. Combine the milk and vanilla extract (the wet ingredients) in a measuring cup.
7. Alternate adding the wet and dry ingredients into the butter mixture until fully combined.
8. Lightly grease a cupcake pan and put in liners; fill ½ - ¾ of each liner with batter.
9. Bake for 8 minutes, rotate the pan, and bake for another 12 minutes.

SUGGESTED FROSTINGS

Don't be scared off by pumpkin cupcakes – a lot of people are! Keep in mind that pumpkin is just another way to sweeten your cupcake with a unique flavor that can be balanced out by cinnamon or cream cheese, and tastes amazing.

TIP *Tangy cream cheese frosting compliments the sweet pumpkin. Snickerdoodle adds cinnamon-y spice.*

PUMPKINCUPCAKES

Makes 12 cupcakes

INGREDIENTS

- ¾ cup softened unsalted butter
- 1 cup sugar
- ½ cup packed light brown sugar
- 1 egg
- ⅔ cup and ¼ cup canned pumpkin
- 1 cup all purpose flour
- 1 ¼ teaspoons baking powder
- 1 teaspoon cinnamon
- ¼ teaspoon salt
- ½ teaspoon vanilla

DIRECTIONS

1. Preheat the oven to 350°F.
2. Whip the butter and the sugar.
3. Crack the egg into a small, separate bowl and add to the butter/sugar mixture.
4. Add the canned pumpkin.
5. Combine the flour, baking powder, cinnamon, and salt in a separate bowl and add to the mixture.
6. Add the vanilla.
7. Lightly grease a cupcake pan and put in liners; fill ½ - ¾ of each liner with batter.
8. Bake for 8 minutes, rotate the pan, and bake for another 11 minutes.

SUGGESTED FROSTINGS

Cream Cheese.......... 54

Snickerdoodle.......... 54

A few years ago, I had been intrigued by some recipes I saw on Pinterest for salted caramel cupcakes, and wanted to start from scratch with my own recipe. At first, I worried that the already-cooked pretzels would burn in the oven (which is what happened to my cookies when I first attempted cookies 'n' cream cupcakes). But, they turned out great, with the pretzels adding the perfect amount of saltiness and texture to the cupcakes.

CARAMELPRETZELCUPCAKES

Makes 12 cupcakes

INGREDIENTS

- ¾ cup softened unsalted butter
- ½ cup sugar
- ½ cup packed light brown sugar
- 2 eggs
- 1 cup all purpose flour
- ⅔ cup crushed pretzels
- 1 ¼ teaspoons baking powder
- ½ teaspoon salt
- ¼ cup whole milk
- ½ teaspoon vanilla extract

DIRECTIONS

1. Preheat the oven to 350°F.
2. Whip the butter and add the sugars.
3. Crack the eggs into a small, separate bowl and add to the butter/sugar mixture.
4. Combine the flour, pretzels, baking powder, and salt (the dry ingredients) in a separate bowl.
5. Combine the milk and vanilla extract (the wet ingredients) in a measuring cup.
6. Alternate adding the wet and dry ingredients into the butter mixture until fully combined.
7. Lightly grease a cupcake pan and put in liners; fill ½ - ¾ of each liner with batter.
8. Bake for 8 minutes, rotate the pan, and bake for another 9 minutes.

SUGGESTED FROSTING

Caramel.................. 52

TIP *Save some graham cracker pieces and sprinkle them over the frosting for a full s'mores effect.*

I wanted to find a way to make a s'mores cupcake by integrating graham crackers into a chocolate cupcake and topping it with marshmallow frosting. First, I experimented with sprinkling some graham cracker crumbs onto the cupcakes before putting them in the oven. I had seen this technique on Instagram before. This works fine, but I prefer mixing the graham cracker chunks in with the butter in the beginning, and then sprinkling the extra crumbs over the top of the cupcakes before they go into the oven.

S'MORES CUPCAKES

Makes 12 cupcakes

INGREDIENTS

- ¾ cup softened unsalted butter
- 1 cup sugar
- 1 cup coarse graham cracker crumbs
- 1 egg
- 1 cup all purpose flour
- 1 ¼ teaspoons baking powder
- ¼ teaspoon salt
- 1 cup cocoa powder
- ½ cup whole milk
- 1 teaspoon vanilla extract

DIRECTIONS

1. Preheat the oven to 350°F.
2. Whip the butter.
3. Add the sugar and graham cracker crumbs.
4. Crack the egg into a small, separate bowl then add it.
5. Combine the flour, baking powder, salt, and cocoa powder (the dry ingredients) in a separate bowl.
6. Combine the milk and vanilla extract (the wet ingredients) in a measuring cup.
7. Alternate adding the wet and dry ingredients.
8. Lightly grease a cupcake pan and put in liners; fill ½ - ¾ of each liner with batter.
9. Bake for 8 minutes, rotate the pan, and bake for another 11 minutes.

SUGGESTED FROSTING

Marshmallow............ 52

TIP *If you like a stronger lemon flavor, add a bit of lemon extract to the frosting.*

The lemon cupcake recipe was actually the fist recipe I decided to recreate from my menu. It took two tries. The first batch of cupcakes stuck to the cupcake wrappers when you tried to pull them apart because I used too much butter. The second time, I used less butter, and it worked!

LEMONCUPCAKES
Makes 12 cupcakes

INGREDIENTS
- ¾ cup softened unsalted butter
- 1 cup sugar
- 1 egg
- 1 cup flour
- 1 ¼ teaspoons baking powder
- ¼ teaspoon salt
- ¼ cup lemon juice
- ½ teaspoon vanilla extract

DIRECTIONS
1. Preheat the oven to 350°F.
2. Whip the butter.
3. Add the sugar.
4. Crack the egg into a small, separate bowl then add it.
5. Combine the flour, baking powder, and salt (the dry ingredients) in a separate bowl.
6. Combine the lemon juice and vanilla extract (the wet ingredients) in a measuring cup.
7. Alternate adding the dry and the wet ingredients.
8. Lightly grease a cupcake pan and put in liners; fill ½ - ¾ of each liner with batter.
9. Bake for 7 minutes, rotate the pan, and bake for another 20 minutes.

SUGGESTED FROSTINGS

TIP

Dye the frosting a pale green (as in the photo) for the full mint effect.

These cupcakes aren't for everyone, as they have three strong flavors in them – coffee, chocolate and mint. However, if you like these flavors, these cupcakes are for you! Also, they are perfect for the holidays. The cupcakes themselves are extremely rich, and the mint frosting adds a nice light touch.

MOCHA MINT CUPCAKES

Makes 12 cupcakes

INGREDIENTS

- ¾ cup softened unsalted butter
- 1 cup sugar
- 1 egg
- 1 cup all purpose flour
- 1 teaspoon baking powder
- ¼ teaspoon salt
- ½ cup cocoa powder
- ¾ cup whole milk
- 1 ½ teaspoons espresso powder

DIRECTIONS

1. Preheat the oven to 350°F.
2. Whip the butter.
3. Add the sugar.
4. Crack the egg into a small, separate bowl then add it.
5. Combine the flour, baking powder, salt, and cocoa powder (the dry ingredients) in a separate bowl.
6. Combine the espresso powder with the milk (the wet ingredients) in a measuring cup.
7. Alternate adding the wet and dry ingredients into the butter mixture.
8. Lightly grease a cupcake pan and put in liners; fill ½ - ¾ of each liner with batter.
9. Bake for 8 minutes, rotate the pan, and bake for another 7 minutes.

SUGGESTED FROSTING

TIP 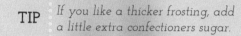 *If you like a thicker frosting, add a little extra confectioners sugar.*

Red Velvet cupcakes are a mystery to people, and they were to me before I started making them. What I found out when I made them for the first time is that they have cocoa in them and taste like a light chocolate. The "red" part of red velvet is actually just food dye.

RED VELVET CUPCAKES

Makes 12 cupcakes

INGREDIENTS

- ¾ cup softened unsalted butter
- 1 cup sugar
- 1 egg
- 1 cup all purpose flour
- ¼ cup cocoa powder
- 1 teaspoon baking powder
- ¼ teaspoon salt
- ¼ cup whole milk
- 1 teaspoon vanilla extract
- 1 tablespoon red gel food dye

DIRECTIONS

1. Preheat the oven to 350°F.
2. Whip the butter.
3. Add the sugar.
4. Crack the egg into a small, separate bowl then add it.
5. Combine the flour, cocoa powder, baking powder, and salt (the dry ingredients) in a separate bowl.
6. Combine the milk and vanilla extract (the wet ingredients) in a measuring cup.
7. Alternate adding the wet and dry ingredients.
8. Add the red gel food dye.
9. Refrigerate the batter for 15 minutes.
10. Lightly grease a cupcake pan and put in liners; fill ½ - ¾ of each liner with batter.
11. Bake for 8 minutes, rotate the pan, bake for another 10 minutes.

SUGGESTED FROSTING

Cream Cheese.......... *54*

Snickerdoodle cupcakes are not familiar to most people, but I wanted to incorporate this recipe into my book because it's a big hit on my menu. The cinnamon-sugar flavor is impossible to resist!

SNICKERDOODLECUPCAKES

Makes 12 cupcakes

INGREDIENTS

- ¾ cup softened unsalted butter
- ½ cup sugar
- ½ cup packed light brown sugar
- 1 egg
- 1 cup all purpose flour
- 1 teaspoon baking powder
- ¼ teaspoon salt
- 1 teaspoon cinnamon
- ¼ cup whole milk
- 1 teaspoon vanilla extract

DIRECTIONS

1. Preheat the oven to 350°F.
2. Whip the butter.
3. Add both sugars.
4. Crack the egg into a small, separate bowl then add it.
5. Combine the flour, baking powder, salt, and cinnamon (the dry ingredients) in a separate bowl.
6. Combine the milk and vanilla extract (the wet ingredients) in a measuring cup.
7. Alternate adding the wet and dry ingredients.
8. Lightly grease a cupcake pan and put in liners; fill ½ - ¾ of each liner with batter.
9. Bake for 8 minutes, rotate the pan, bake for another 10 minutes.

SUGGESTED FROSTING

Snickerdoodle.......... 54

This recipe is popular with people of all ages. Something to keep in mind is that when crushing up the cookies for the cupcake batter, you can leave larger chunks. But, for the frosting, you really want to crush up the cookies into a powder because otherwise, the chunks get stuck in the piping tip and cause a big mess.

COOKIES 'N' CREAM CUPCAKES

Makes 12 cupcakes

INGREDIENTS

- ¾ cup softened unsalted butter
- 1 cup sugar
- 1 egg
- 1 cup all purpose flour
- 1 teaspoon baking powder
- ¼ teaspoon salt
- 2 tablespoons coarsely crushed chocolate cookies (like the cookie part of Oreos™)
- ¼ cup whole milk
- 1 teaspoon vanilla

DIRECTIONS

1. Preheat the oven to 350°F.
2. Whip the butter.
3. Add the sugar.
4. Crack the egg into a small, separate bowl then add it.
5. Combine the flour, baking powder, salt, and crushed cookies (the dry ingredients) in a separate bowl.
6. Combine the milk and vanilla extract (the wet ingredients) in a measuring cup.
7. Alternate adding the wet and dry ingredients to the butter mixture.
8. Lightly grease a cupcake pan and put in liners; fill ½ - ¾ of each liner with batter.
9. Bake for 8 minutes, rotate the pan, bake for another 9 minutes.

SUGGESTED FROSTING

Cookies 'n' Cream... 55

Vanilla.................. 50

TIP *Try chocolate frosting for a mocha flavor.*

These cupcakes are more popular with adults than younger kids (for obvious reasons). Though they have a strong coffee flavor, it's not too overpowering, so the cupcakes still taste sweet.

COFFEECUPCAKES

Makes 12 cupcakes

INGREDIENTS

- ¾ cup softened unsalted butter
- ½ cup sugar
- ½ cup packed light brown sugar
- 1 egg
- 1 cup all purpose flour
- 1 ¼ teaspoons baking powder
- ¼ teaspoon salt
- 1 ½ teaspoons espresso powder
- ¼ cup whole milk
- 1 teaspoon vanilla extract

DIRECTIONS

1. Preheat the oven to 350°F.
2. Whip the butter.
3. Add both sugars.
4. Crack the egg into a small, separate bowl then add it.
5. Combine the flour, baking powder, salt, and espresso powder (the dry ingredients) in a separate bowl.
6. Combine the milk and vanilla extract (the wet ingredients) in a measuring cup.
7. Alternate adding the wet and dry ingredients.
8. Lightly grease a cupcake pan and put in liners; fill ½ - ¾ of each liner with batter.
9. Bake for 8 minutes, rotate the pan, and bake for another 10 minutes.

SUGGESTED FROSTING

Coffee.................... 55

Chocolate............... 50

Coconut is not a flavor that is present in most people's daily life like chocolate and vanilla are. But, I was scrolling around a lot on Pinterest when I got the inspiration to create this cupcake. I think it's absolutely delicious and gives coconut its moment to shine.

COCONUT CUPCAKES

Makes 12 cupcakes

INGREDIENTS

- ¾ cup softened unsalted butter
- 1 cup sugar
- 2 eggs
- 1 cup all purpose flour
- 1 ¼ teaspoons baking powder
- ¾ cup packed sweetened shredded coconut
- ¼ cup whole milk
- ½ teaspoon vanilla extract

DIRECTIONS

1. Preheat the oven to 350°F.
2. Whip the butter.
3. Add the sugar and eggs.
4. Combine the flour, baking powder, and shredded coconut (the dry ingredients) in a separate bowl.
5. Combine the milk and vanilla extract (the wet ingredients) in a measuring cup.
6. Alternate adding the wet and dry ingredients.
7. Lightly grease a cupcake pan and put in liners; fill ½ - ¾ of each liner with batter.
8. Bake for 8 minutes, rotate the pan, and bake for another 12 minutes.

SUGGESTED FROSTING

Coconut.................. 57

For these cupcakes, incorporating maple into them was an easy task, but getting the bacon into the batter proved impossible – the bacon would never cook properly. The solution I finally came up with – garnishing the cupcakes with the bacon – still allows for both flavors to be present, delicious, and fully cooked through.

MAPLEBACONCUPCAKES
Makes 12 cupcakes

INGREDIENTS
- 1 package bacon
- ¾ cup softened unsalted butter
- ½ cup sugar
- ½ cup packed light brown sugar
- 2 eggs
- 1 cup flour
- 1 ¼ teaspoons baking powder
- ¼ teaspoon salt
- 2 tablespoons maple syrup

DIRECTIONS
1. Preheat the oven to 350°F.
2. Place the bacon strips on a cooling rack on top of a cookie pan and place in the oven for 30 minutes or until your desired level of crispiness.
3. Whip the butter until fluffy.
4. Add both sugars.
5. Crack eggs into a small, separate bowl then add them to the butter/sugar mixture.
6. Combine the flour, baking powder, and salt in a separate bowl and add.
7. Pour the maple syrup into the mixture and mix thoroughly.
8. Lightly grease a cupcake pan and put in liners; fill ½ - ¾ of each liner with batter.
9. Bake cupcakes for 10 minutes, rotate the pan, and bake for another 20 minutes.
10. Chop up the bacon into small bits and sprinkle over the frosting.

SUGGESTED FROSTING

These cupcakes have a lot of ingredients but the final result is worth it! All of the different flavors complement each other very nicely. Even if you think you don't like carrot cake, step out of your comfort zone because these cupcakes are sweet and delicious!

CARROTCAKECUPCAKES

Makes 12 cupcakes

INGREDIENTS

- ¾ cup softened unsalted butter
- ½ cup sugar
- ½ cup packed light brown sugar
- 2 eggs
- 1 ½ cups all purpose flour
- 1 ¼ teaspoons baking powder
- ¼ teaspoon salt
- 2 cups grated carrots
- ¾ cup packed sweetened shredded coconut
- 1 cup shelled walnuts

DIRECTIONS

1. Preheat the oven to 350°F.
2. Whip the butter.
3. Add both sugars.
4. Crack the eggs into a small, separate bowl then add them.
5. Combine the flour, baking powder, and salt (the dry ingredients) in a separate bowl and add.
6. Add the carrots, coconut, and walnuts to the butter mixture.
7. Add the dry ingredients.
8. Lightly grease a cupcake pan and put in liners; fill ½ - ¾ of each liner with batter.
9. Bake for 8 minutes, rotate the pan, and bake for another 15 minutes.

SUGGESTED FROSTING

Cream Cheese.......... 54

FROSTING

VANILLA FROSTING

INGREDIENTS
- 1 cup softened unsalted butter
- 1 pound and ¾ cups confectioners sugar
- ¼ cup whole milk
- 1 teaspoon vanilla extract

DIRECTIONS
1. Whip the butter.
2. Add the sugar slowly.
3. Combine the milk and vanilla extract in a measuring cup then add it to the butter/sugar mixture.

CHOCOLATE FROSTING

INGREDIENTS
- 2 cups softened unsalted butter
- 1 pound confectioners sugar
- 2 cups melted milk chocolate chips (melted at 15 second increments in the microwave).

DIRECTIONS
1. Whip the butter.
2. Add the sugar.
3. Whip the chocolate chips with a spatula until no lumps of chocolate remain and add to the butter mixture.

This caramel frosting is packed full of brown sugar and butter, and you might notice that the frosting is not 100% smooth. This is because most frostings use just confectioners sugar, but for a delicious caramel taste, brown sugar is a must for this recipe.

CARAMELFROSTING

INGREDIENTS

- ½ cup softened unsalted butter
- ¾ cup packed light brown sugar
- 1 pound confectioners sugar
- ¼ cup and 1 teaspoon whole milk

DIRECTIONS

1. Beat the butter and light brown sugar together.
2. Add the confectioners sugar and the milk.

MARSHMALLOWFROSTING

INGREDIENTS

- 1 cup softened unsalted butter
- 3 cups marshmallow fluff
- 1 pound confectioners sugar
- 1 teaspoon vanilla extract

DIRECTIONS

1. Combine the butter and marshmallow fluff.
2. Add the confectioners sugar.
3. Add the vanilla extract.

LEMON FROSTING

INGREDIENTS
- 1 cup softened unsalted butter
- 2 pounds confectioners sugar
- ⅔ cup whole milk
- 4 teaspoons lemon zest
- 1 teaspoon lemon extract (optional)

DIRECTIONS
1. Combine the butter and confectioners sugar.
2. Add the milk.
3. Add the lemon zest.
4. For a stronger lemon flavor, add lemon extract.

MINT FROSTING

INGREDIENTS
- 1 cup softened unsalted butter
- 2 pounds confectioners sugar
- ½ cup whole milk
- ½ teaspoon vanilla extract
- 1 teaspoon peppermint extract

DIRECTIONS
1. Combine the butter and confectioners sugar.
2. Combine the milk and vanilla extract in a measuring cup.
3. Add the milk mixture and the peppermint extract.

CREAMCHEESEFROSTING

INGREDIENTS
- ½ cup softened unsalted butter
- ¾ cup room temperature cream cheese
- 1 pound and 1 cup confectioners sugar
- 2 teaspoons vanilla extract
- ¼ cup whole milk

DIRECTIONS
1. Combine the butter and cream cheese.
2. Slowly add the confectioners sugar.
3. Add the vanilla extract.
4. Add the milk.

SNICKERDOODLEFROSTING

INGREDIENTS
- 2 cups softened unsalted butter
- 2 pounds confectioners sugar
- 2 teaspoons cinnamon
- ½ cup whole milk
- 2 teaspoons vanilla extract

DIRECTIONS
1. Whip the butter.
2. Slowly add the sugar.
3. Add the cinnamon.
4. Combine the milk and vanilla extract in a measuring cup then add it.

COOKIES N CREAM FROSTING

INGREDIENTS
- 1 cup softened unsalted butter
- 1 pound confectioners sugar
- 1 tablespoon finely crushed chocolate cookies (like the cookie part of Oreos™)
- ¼ cup whole milk
- 1 teaspoon vanilla extract

DIRECTIONS
1. Whip the butter.
2. Slowly add the confectioners sugar.
3. Add the finely crushed cookies.
4. Combine the milk and vanilla extract in a measuring cup and add it.

COFFEE FROSTING

INGREDIENTS
- 1 cup softened unsalted butter
- 1 pound and 1 ¼ cup confectioners sugar
- 2 teaspoons espresso powder
- ½ cup whole milk
- 1 teaspoon vanilla extract

DIRECTIONS
1. Whip the butter.
2. Slowly add the confectioners sugar.
3. Add the espresso powder.
4. Combine the milk and vanilla extract in a measuring cup then add it.
5. Add the milk mixture to the butter mixture.

Dehydrated raspberries are the key to this tart frosting. Perfect on lemon cupcakes!

COCONUT FROSTING

INGREDIENTS

- 1 cup softened unsalted butter
- 1 pound and 1 cup confectioners sugar
- ½ cup coconut milk
- ¼ cup packed sweetened shredded coconut

DIRECTIONS

1. Whip the butter.
2. Slowly add the confectioners sugar.
3. Add the coconut milk and the shredded coconut.

RASPBERRY FROSTING

INGREDIENTS

- 1 cup softened unsalted butter
- 1 cup finely crushed dehydrated raspberries
- 1 cup confectioners sugar
- ¼ cup whole milk

DIRECTIONS

1. Whip the butter.
2. Slowly add the confectioners sugar and the crushed raspberries.
3. Add the milk to the mixture.

MAPLEFROSTING

INGREDIENTS
- 1 cup softened unsalted butter
- 1 pound and ¾ cup confectioners sugar
- 3 tablespoons whole milk
- 5 tablespoons and 1 teaspoon maple syrup (the less viscous, the better)

DIRECTIONS
1. Whip the butter.
2. Slowly add the confectioners sugar.
3. Add the milk and the syrup.

ASSEMBLINGAPIPINGBAG

Coupler Collar Tip

1. Put the coupler inside the pastry bag and cut off the plastic bit in front of it.

2. Place the tip on top of the coupler and over the bag.

3. Place the collar over the tip, sandwiching the tip between the coupler and the collar. Screw the collar on.

4. Place frosting into the piping bag. My favorite method is to put the assembled bag tip-down into a cup; fold the bag over the rim and spatula the frosting in.

5. Twist the top and your piping bag is ready to go!

PIPINGACUPCAKE

Follow these steps for the perfect frosting swirl on your cupcakes.

1. Pipe a small dollop in the center of the cupcake to hold up the rest of the swirl.

2. Start from the side of the cupcake and make a full circle of frosting.

3. Once you have gone around the cupcake one full time, go around again on top of the first layer of frosting. Pipe inwards so that your frosting rests against the initial dollop in the middle.

4. Once you have swirled the cupcake about three times, apply NO pressure to the piping bag and lift up quickly for the perfect final point.

COOKIES

These cookies have always been one of my biggest hits, but until recently I was using a different recipe. I wanted to make the cookies crispier but wasn't sure how. My mom suggested adding more butter, and the cookies thinned out and became crispy, but not brittle or burnt. They are absolutely delicious!

CHOCOLATECHIPCOOKIES

Makes 24 cookies

INGREDIENTS

- ¾ cup melted unsalted butter
- ½ cup sugar
- ½ cup packed light brown sugar
- 1 ⅛ cups all purpose flour
- ½ teaspoon baking soda
- ¼ teaspoon salt
- 1 egg
- 1 teaspoon vanilla extract
- ½ bag milk chocolate chips

DIRECTIONS

1. Preheat the oven to 375°F.
2. Add both sugars to the melted unsalted butter.
3. Combine the flour, baking soda, and salt (the dry ingredients) in a separate bowl.
4. Whisk the egg with a fork and add the vanilla extract in a separate bowl.
5. Add the butter mixture and the egg mixture to the dry ingredients.
6. Add the chocolate chips.
7. Refrigerate the dough for at least 30 minutes.
8. Line your baking sheet(s) with parchment paper.
9. Scoop a heaping tablespoon of dough and form into a ball; place no more than 9 balls on each baking sheet, and flatten them out slightly.
10. Bake for 10 minutes.

These cookies tend to be a bit crumbly, so beware when you are serving them. They are a sweet, wholesome cookie that appeals to adults and kids alike.

OATMEALRAISINCOOKIES
Makes 24 cookies

INGREDIENTS

- 1 ¼ cups softened unsalted butter
- ½ cup packed light brown sugar
- 1 egg
- ½ teaspoon baking soda
- ¾ cup all purpose flour
- 1 ½ cups old fashioned oats
- 1 teaspoon cinnamon
- ½ teaspoon salt
- 1 cup raisins

DIRECTIONS

1. Preheat the oven to 375°F.
2. Combine the butter and sugar.
3. Crack the egg into a small, separate bowl and add it to the mixing bowl.
4. Combine the baking soda, flour, oats, cinnamon, and salt in a separate bowl and add to the butter mixture.
5. Add the raisins to the mixture.
6. Line your baking sheet(s) with parchment paper.
7. Scoop a heaping tablespoon of dough and form into a ball; place no more than 9 balls on each baking sheet, and flatten them out slightly.
8. Bake for 10 minutes.

I decided to call this recipe "brown sugar cookies" but they could also be called "caramel cookies." I think that brown sugar, which I use in lots of my recipes, is the happy medium between the simple, sweet flavor of traditional sugar cookies, and the rich, creamy flavor of caramel.

BROWNSUGARCOOKIES

Makes 24 cookies

INGREDIENTS

- 1 cup softened unsalted butter
- ¼ cup sugar
- ¾ cup packed light brown sugar
- 1 egg
- 1 ½ cups flour
- 1 teaspoon baking soda
- ¼ teaspoon salt
- 1 teaspoon vanilla

DIRECTIONS

1. Preheat the over to 375°F.
2. Whip the butter and add both sugars.
3. Crack the egg into a small, separate bowl then add it to the mixing bowl.
4. Combine the flour, baking soda, and salt in a separate bowl and add to the mixing bowl.
5. Add the vanilla extract.
6. Line your baking sheet(s) with parchment paper.
7. Scoop a heaping tablespoon of dough and form into a ball; place no more than 9 balls on each baking sheet, and flatten them out slightly.
8. Bake for 10 minutes.

I wanted to include lemon cookies in my cookbook for one reason: people who love lemon *really* love lemon, and I thought it would only be fair – seeing as I am one of those people – to include this recipe in my book.

LEMONCOOKIES

Makes 24 cookies

INGREDIENTS

- 1 cup softened unsalted butter
- 1 cup sugar
- 1 egg
- 1 ½ cups flour
- ½ teaspoon baking soda
- ¼ teaspoon salt
- 3 teaspoons lemon zest
- 2 tablespoons lemon juice

DIRECTIONS

1. Preheat the oven to 375°F.
2. Whip the butter.
3. Add the sugar.
4. Crack the egg into a small, separate bowl then add it to the mixing bowl.
5. Combine the flour, baking soda, and salt (the dry ingredients) in a separate bowl.
6. Mix the lemon zest with the lemon juice in a measuring cup.
7. Alternate adding the wet and dry ingredients to the mixing bowl.
8. Line your baking sheet(s) with parchment paper.
9. Scoop a heaping tablespoon of dough and form into a ball; place no more than 9 balls on each baking sheet, and flatten them out slightly.
10. Bake for 10 minutes.

These cookies have the perfect level of peanut butter flavor in them – it's enough to taste it, but not too much that it's overwhelming. And they are deliciously crumbly!

PEANUTBUTTERCOOKIES

Makes 24 cookies

INGREDIENTS

- 1 cup softened unsalted butter
- ¾ cup creamy peanut butter
- 1 egg
- ½ cup sugar
- 1 cup all purpose flour
- ½ teaspoon baking soda
- ¼ teaspoon salt

DIRECTIONS

1. Preheat the oven to 375°F.
2. Whip the butter and peanut butter together.
3. Crack the egg into a small, separate bowl then add it to the mixing bowl.
4. Add the sugar.
5. Combine the flour, baking soda, and salt in a separate bowl and add to the mixing bowl.
6. Refrigerate the dough for 20 minutes minimum.
7. Line your baking sheet(s) with parchment paper.
8. Scoop a heaping tablespoon of dough and form into a ball; place no more than 9 balls on each baking sheet, and flatten them out slightly.
9. Bake for 10 minutes.

I kicked up my peanut butter cookie recipe by adding chocolate chips for a classic flavor combination.

CHOCOLATE
PEANUTBUTTERCOOKIES

Makes 24 cookies

INGREDIENTS

- 1 cup softened unsalted butter
- ¾ cup creamy peanut butter
- 1 egg
- ½ cup sugar
- 1 cup all purpose flour
- ½ teaspoon baking soda
- ¼ teaspoon salt
- ½ bag milk chocolate chips

DIRECTIONS

1. Preheat the oven to 375°F.
2. Whip the butter and peanut butter together.
3. Crack the egg into a small, separate bowl then add it to the mixing bowl
4. Add the sugar.
5. Combine the flour, baking soda, and salt in a separate bowl and add to the mixing bowl.
6. Add the chocolate chips.
7. Refrigerate the dough for at least 20 minutes.
8. Line your baking sheet(s) with parchment paper.
9. Scoop a heaping tablespoon of dough and form into a ball; place no more than 9 balls on each baking sheet, and flatten them out slightly.
10. Bake for 10 minutes.

TREATS

The truffle recipe I used to make for my menu was so complicated and time consuming that I decided to completely simplify it for my book. This is one of the easiest recipes I make, but also one of the most delicious.

COCOAHAZELNUTTRUFFLES

Makes 16 truffles

INGREDIENTS

- 1 ½ cups cocoa hazelnut spread (like Nutella™)
- 1 cup all purpose flour
- 1 cup confectioners sugar

DIRECTIONS

1. Line a baking sheet with parchment paper.
2. Combine the chocolate hazelnut spread and the flour.
3. Roll the mixture into small balls.
4. Sift confectioners sugar over truffles.
5. Refrigerate until ready to serve.

If you make these brownies, be prepared to experience chocolate in a whole new way! These brownies are so packed to the brim with cocoa powder and chocolate chips that you should be sure to have a glass of milk ready when you eat them.

BROWNIES

Makes 12 brownies

INGREDIENTS

- 2 cups softened unsalted butter
- 2 cups sugar
- 2 eggs
- 3 cups cocoa powder
- 2 ½ cups flour
- 2 ½ teaspoons baking powder
- ½ cup whole milk
- 2 teaspoons vanilla
- 1 bag milk chocolate chips

DIRECTIONS

1. Preheat the oven to 375°F.
2. Combine the cocoa powder, flour, and baking powder (the dry ingredients) in a bowl.
3. Combine the milk and vanilla extract (the wet ingredients) in a measuring cup.
4. Crack the eggs into a small, separate bowl.
5. Whip the butter and add the sugar in a large separate bowl.
6. Add the eggs to the butter mixture.
7. Alternate adding the wet and dry ingredients into the butter mixture.
8. Add the chocolate chips.
9. Grease a 9"x13" baking pan with butter, oil, or cooking spray and line the bottom with parchment paper. Pour into the pan.
10. Bake for 23 minutes.
11. Let cool then cut into 12 brownies.

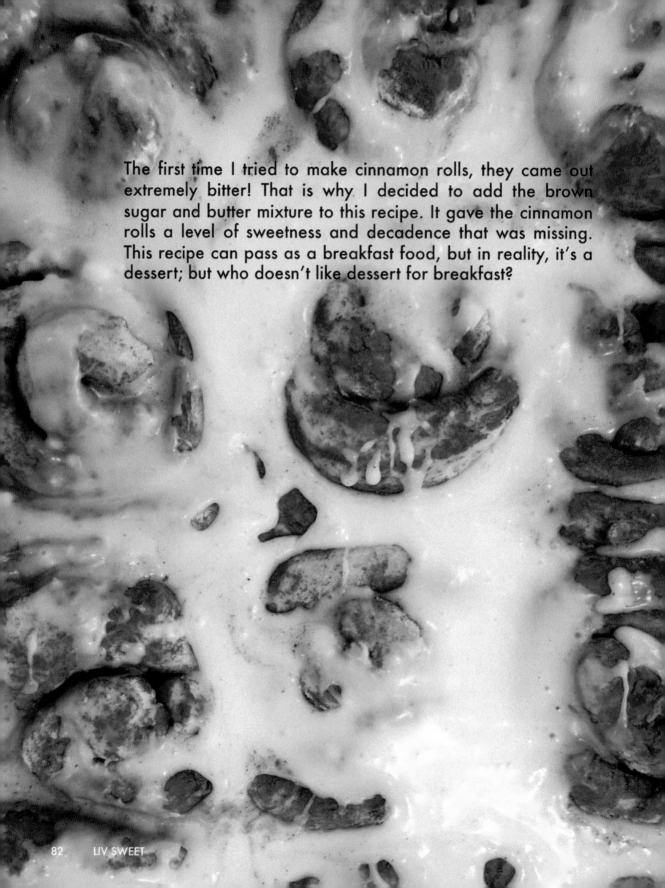

The first time I tried to make cinnamon rolls, they came out extremely bitter! That is why I decided to add the brown sugar and butter mixture to this recipe. It gave the cinnamon rolls a level of sweetness and decadence that was missing. This recipe can pass as a breakfast food, but in reality, it's a dessert; but who doesn't like dessert for breakfast?

MINICINNAMONROLLS
Makes 12 rolls

ROLLS INGREDIENTS

- ¾ cup warm water
- 1 packet active dry yeast
- 2 ¾ cups all purpose flour
- ¾ cup sugar
- ¼ cup whole milk
- ¼ cup confectioners sugar
- 2 tablespoons cinnamon
- ½ cup unsalted butter
- ¾ cup packed light brown sugar

GLAZE INGREDIENTS

- 2 cups confectioners sugar
- 4 tablespoons water

DIRECTIONS

1. Preheat the oven to 375°F.
2. Sprinkle the active dry yeast over the warm water and set aside for 5 minutes.
3. Combine the flour and sugar in a separate mixing bowl.
4. Add the water mixture.
5. Add the milk to the mixture.
6. Flour your surfaces and roll out the dough.
7. Cut 12 equal strips.
8. Melt the butter over a stove and add the light brown sugar.
9. Once the butter starts to boil, turn off the heat and mix until the brown sugar is completely combined with the butter.

(recipe continues on next page)

DIRECTIONS *(continued)*

10. Combine the confectioners sugar and the cinnamon in a separate bowl and spread this mixture over the strips of dough.

11. Once the brown sugar mixture has cooled for a few minutes, spread it over the strips of dough.

12. Roll up the strips of dough making sure to keep as much of the cinnamon and brown sugar mixtures inside of the roll.

13. Place the rolls onto a well greased pan and bake for 15 minutes.

14. For the glaze, combine the confectioners sugar and the water.

15. Pour the glaze over the cinnamon rolls one minute after they come out of the oven.

This recipe is another simple one that is absolutely delicious! When refrigerating the bars, do not expect the peanut butter to become solid— this adds to the effect! Biting into the thin, hardened layer of chocolate and then into the smooth, creamy peanut butter is absolutely perfect.

CHOCOLATEPEANUT BUTTERBARS

Makes 12 bars

CRUST INGREDIENTS

- ¾ cup melted unsalted butter
- ½ cup sugar
- ½ cup packed light brown sugar
- 1 ⅛ cups all purpose flour
- ½ teaspoon baking soda
- ¼ teaspoon salt
- 1 egg
- 1 teaspoon vanilla extract
- ½ bag milk chocolate chips

TOPPING INGREDIENTS

- 4 cups creamy peanut butter
- 1 bag milk chocolate chips (melted in a microwave-safe bowl in 15-second increments)
- Chopped up peanut butter cups (optional)

DIRECTIONS

1. Preheat the oven to 375°F.
2. Add both sugars to the melted unsalted butter.
3. Combine the flour, baking soda, and salt (the dry ingredients) in a separate bowl.
4. In another bowl, whisk the egg with a fork and add the vanilla extract.
5. Add the butter mixture and the egg mixture to the dry ingredients.
6. Add the chocolate chips and refrigerate the dough for at least 30 minutes.

DIRECTIONS *(continued)*

7. Line your baking sheet with parchment paper and form the dough on the baking sheet into a large rectangle.

8. Bake for 13 minutes.

9. Allow the chocolate chip cookie crust to cool for a few minutes and spread the peanut butter on evenly.

10. Once the peanut butter and crust are cooled, spread on the melted chocolate chips.

11. If you choose to use the peanut butter cups, sprinkle them on before the chocolate sets so they stick.

12. Place in refrigerator for at least 30 minutes then cut into 12 pieces.

Lemon bars are one of the biggest hits on my menu, so I knew I needed to include them in this book. They get their amazing lemon flavor from freshly zested and squeezed lemons, so using fresh lemons is one of the most important steps in making these delicious lemon bars!

LEMONBARS

Makes 12 bars

CRUST INGREDIENTS

- 1 ½ cups all purpose flour
- ½ cup cornstarch
- ½ cup confectioners sugar
- ⅛ teaspoon salt
- 1 cup softened unsalted butter

FILLING INGREDIENTS

- 4 eggs
- 2 tablespoons and 1 teaspoon lemon zest
- ⅔ cup lemon juice
- 1 ½ cups sugar
- ¼ cup all purpose flour

DIRECTIONS

1. Mix all of the ingredients for the crust together.
2. Flatten out the dough for the crust onto a well greased baking pan. The dough should only take up half of the pan.
3. Preheat the oven to 350°F.
4. Refrigerate the dough in the pan for at least 20 minutes.
5. Bake the dough for 22 minutes.
6. While the crust is in the oven, make the filling.
7. Mix all of the ingredients for the filling together.
8. Once you take the crust out of the oven, let it cool for 5 minutes, and then pour on the filling. Allow the filling to spill over the entire baking sheet.
9. Bake again for 25 minutes.
10. Once cooled, spread the filling over the cookie base, sift some confectioners sugar over the top (optional) then cut into 12 bars.

A few years ago, an edible/eggless cookie dough craze hit my class. Many people, including myself, ordered it online, but I knew I could make this delicious and of-the-moment treat myself. I took my regular chocolate chip cookie recipe, changed a few ingredients, and made the perfect eggless cookie dough!

EDIBLECOOKIEDOUGH

Makes 1 batch

INGREDIENTS

- ½ cup melted unsalted butter
- ½ cup packed light brown sugar
- ½ cup sugar
- 1 ⅛ cups all purpose flour
- ¼ teaspoon salt
- 1 teaspoon vanilla extract
- ¼ cup buttermilk
- ½ bag milk chocolate chips

DIRECTIONS

1. Combine the butter and sugars.
2. Mix together the flour and salt in a separate bowl and add that mixture to the butter mixture.
3. Combine the vanilla and buttermilk in a measuring cup and add it to the butter mixture.
4. Add the chocolate chips.
5. Make sure to keep refrigerated.

This is the only pie recipe in this cookbook because it's my absolute favorite! It doesn't include any whipped cream because I prefer this pie on its own. Keep in mind that the crust is not supposed to go up the sides; it's only meant to cover the bottom.

KEYLIMEPIE

CRUST INGREDIENTS

- 2 cups coarsely crushed graham crackers
- 2 tablespoons sugar
- 6 tablespoons melted unsalted butter

FILLING INGREDIENTS

- 3 egg yolks
- ⅔ cup lime juice
- 1 ½ cups sweetened condensed milk
- 1 tablespoon and 1 teaspoon lime zest

DIRECTIONS

1. Preheat your oven to 350°F.
2. Mix all of the ingredients for the crust together, and press into the bottom of a well greased pie pan (the best way to grease the pan is with vegetable shortening, but you can use cooking spray as well).
3. Bake for 7 minutes.
4. Whisk together all of the ingredients for the filling.
5. Allow the crust to cool and then pour in the filling; bake for 15 minutes.

TIP *If you can find key limes, use them for this recipe, but regular limes work just as well.*

This recipe is one of the most simple and delicious treats in the book, but it was hard to develop because I didn't realize I needed butter to make it. I kept trying to heat up different quantities of marshmallows and mixing them with cereal, only to end up with a sticky mess! So, do not forget the butter in this recipe! Enjoy!

RICECRISPYTREATS

Makes 12 treats

INGREDIENTS

- ½ cup unsalted butter
- 10 cups mini marshmallows
- 9 cups of crispy rice cereal (like Rice Krispies™)

DIRECTIONS

1. Place a pot over the stove, and begin melting the butter on medium heat.

2. Add the marshmallows to the butter and stir gently until the marshmallows are still lumpy, but mostly soft and melty. Be careful not to burn them.

3. Fold the rice cereal into the marshmallow and butter mixture with a greased spatula.

4. Turn off the heat.

5. Grease a baking sheet and flatten out the mixture on top to your desired thickness.

6. Place in the refrigerator for at least 30 minutes then cut into 12 pieces.

At first my goal for this recipe was to make a chocolatey version of a rice crispy treat. I used cocoa rice crispies and poured melted chocolate on top, placing on mini marshmallows before the chocolate set. This recipe didn't work out because the hardened chocolate base of the bars melted too easily. I then tried with cinnamon cereal, less chocolate, and more melted marshmallows for support: the bars held together and tasted just like I hoped.

S'MORES BARS

Makes 18 bars

INGREDIENTS

- ½ cup unsalted butter
- 10 cups mini marshmallows
- 9 cups of cinnamon cereal (like Cinnamon Toast Crunch™)
- 1 bag milk chocolate chips

DIRECTIONS

1. Place a pot over the stove and begin melting the butter on medium heat.
2. Add the marshmallows to the butter and stir gently until the marshmallows are still lumpy, but mostly soft and melty.
3. Fold in the cinnamon cereal.
4. Turn off the heat.
5. Fold in the chocolate chips (they should not fully melt).
6. Form small balls of your preferred size (mine are about the size of a heaping tablespoon) on a well-greased baking sheet and place in the refrigerator for at least 30 minutes.

I was inspired to make these donuts because I love lemon poppy seed muffins, and I wanted to somehow make them my own. When I got a donut pan for my birthday, I figured out how!

LEMONPOPPYSEEDDONUTS

Makes 12 donuts

DONUT INGREDIENTS

- ¾ cup softened unsalted butter
- 1 cup sugar
- 1 egg
- 1 ½ cups all purpose flour
- 1 ¼ teaspoons baking powder
- ¼ cup poppy seeds
- 3 tablespoons lemon zest
- ¼ cup lemon juice

TIP *For this and other donut recipes, use a donut pan (pictured on page 16).*

GLAZE INGREDIENTS

- 2 cups confectioners sugar
- 4 tablespoons water

DIRECTIONS

1. Preheat the oven to 375°F.
2. Whip the butter and add the sugar.
3. Add the egg.
4. Combine the flour, baking powder, and poppy seeds (the dry ingredients) in a separate bowl.
5. Mix together the lemon juice and the lemon zest (the wet ingredients) in a measuring cup.
6. Alternately add the dry and wet ingredients to the butter mixture.
7. Grease your donut pan well and fill the cavities up halfway.
8. Bake for 10 minutes.
9. While the donuts are in the oven, combine the ingredients for the glaze.
10. Once the donuts have cooled, you may want to cut off anything that has baked into the hole of the donut.
11. Pour on the glaze.

Everything about this recipe just seems to make sense. Everyone knows that people love to eat coffee and donuts together, so why not just make them into one? These donuts have a strong coffee flavor, but still are sweet and delicious.

COFFEEDONUTS
Makes 12 donuts

DONUT INGREDIENTS
- ¾ cup softened unsalted butter
- 1 cup sugar
- 1 egg
- 1 ½ cups all purpose flour
- 1 ¼ teaspoons baking powder
- ¼ cup espresso powder
- ¼ cup whole milk
- 1 teaspoon vanilla

GLAZE INGREDIENTS
- 1 cup and 4 tablespoons confectioners sugar
- 1 teaspoon espresso powder
- 3 tablespoons water

DIRECTIONS
1. Preheat the oven to 375°F.
2. Whip the butter and then add the sugar and the egg.
3. Combine the flour, baking powder, and espresso powder (the dry ingredients) in a separate bowl.
4. Combine the milk and vanilla (the wet ingredients) in a measuring cup.
5. Alternately add the dry and wet ingredients to the butter mixture.
6. Grease your donut pan well and fill the cavities up halfway.
7. Bake for 10 minutes.
8. While the donuts are in the oven, combine the ingredients for the glaze.
9. Once the donuts have cooled, you may want to cut off anything that has baked into the hole of the donut.
10. Pour on the glaze.

TIP *Add a little green food dye to these donuts for effect, and so people know they are mint.*

I love mint chocolate chip flavored treats, and these donuts are no exception!

MINTCHOCOLATECHIP DONUTS

Makes 12 donuts

DONUT INGREDIENTS

- ¾ cup softened unsalted butter
- 1 cup sugar
- 1 egg
- 1 ½ cups all purpose flour
- 1 ¼ teaspoons baking powder
- ¼ cup whole milk
- 1 teaspoon peppermint extract
- ⅓ cup milk chocolate chips
- Green food dye (optional)

GLAZE INGREDIENTS

- 2 cups confectioners sugar
- 4 tablespoons water

DIRECTIONS

1. Preheat the oven to 375°F.
2. Whip the butter and add the sugar and egg.
3. Combine the flour and baking powder (the dry ingredients) in a separate bowl.
4. Combine the milk and peppermint extract in a measuring cup.
5. Alternately add the wet and dry ingredients into the butter mixture.
6. Add the chocolate chips and the food dye.
7. Fill each cavity in your donut pan halfway full.
8. Bake for 10 minutes.
9. While the donuts are in the oven, combine the ingredients for the glaze.
10. Once the donuts have cooled, you may want to cut off anything that has baked into the hole of the donut.
11. Pour on the glaze.

This recipe was extremely hard to create! The cookie part is a hybrid between a cookie and a cupcake, and the filling is a hybrid between frosting and whipped cream. Something different about this recipe from my others is that it uses vegetable oil. I turned to Pinterest and found out almost all whoopie pies get the right texture from oil, which is something I didn't know.

WHOOPIEPIES

Makes 6 Whoopie Pies

COOKIE INGREDIENTS

- 1 ½ cups all purpose flour
- ½ cup cocoa powder
- 1 cup packed light brown sugar
- 1 ¼ teaspoons baking powder
- ¼ teaspoon salt
- 3 eggs
- 1/2 cup vegetable oil
- I teaspoon vanilla extract

FILLING INGREDIENTS

- 2 cups heavy whipping cream
- 4 cups confectioners sugar

DIRECTIONS

1. Preheat oven to 375°F.
2. Combine the flour, cocoa powder, baking powder, and salt in a bowl; add the sugar and then the eggs.
3. Add the oil and vanilla extract.
4. Place the batter in a piping bag and pipe into circles of equal size (I make mine about the size of my fist) onto a baking sheet lined with parchment paper. The batter should have a fairly runny consistency.
5. Bake for 15 minutes.
6. While the cookies are baking, make the filling.
7. Whip the heavy whipping cream until it thickens (about 5 minutes).
8. Add the confectioners sugar.
9. Refrigerate the filling until the cookies have cooled.
10. Pipe the filling onto half of the cookies, and place the other cookies on top.
11. Refrigerate before serving.

This is the only tart recipe in this book because I think they are absolutely delicious. Luckily, you can use this crust for just about any type of tart you would like.

CINNAMONSUGARTARTS

Makes 12 tarts

CRUST INGREDIENTS
- 4 cups all purpose flour
- 1 cup confectioners sugar
- 1 cup softened salted butter, cubed
- ½ cup cold water
- ½ teaspoon salt

FILLING INGREDIENTS
- 4 teaspoons unsalted butter
- 1 cup packed light brown sugar
- 1 ½ teaspoons cinnamon

GLAZE INGREDIENTS
- 2 cups confectioners sugar
- 4 tablespoons water
- ½ teaspoon cinnamon

DIRECTIONS
1. Preheat the oven to 350°F.
2. Combine all of the ingredients for the crust.
3. Mix with your hands by scrunching the dough together until just combined. (Do not overmix!)
4. Flour your surface; role out the dough then cut into equally-sized rectangles.
5. Line your baking sheet(s) with parchment paper and line up half of your rectangles.
6. For the filling, place the ingredients in a pot over the stove at medium heat and stir until fully combined. Remove from stove.
7. Once the filling has cooled for a few minutes, spoon it into the middle of your rectangles.
8. Place the other rectangles on top of the filling, and press the sides closed with a fork.
9. Poke a few small holes on the top of the tarts.
10. Bake for 15 minutes.

DECORATION

RULESOFSPRINKLES

Abiding by the following rules while decorating
will ensure an elegant look.

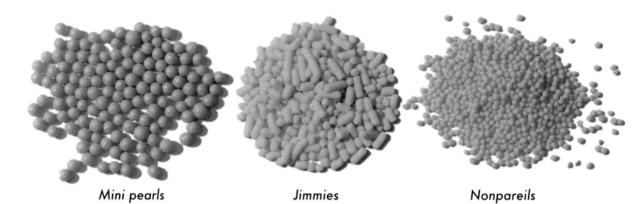

Mini pearls *Jimmies* *Nonpareils*

1. Don't use colored nonpareils with rainbow nonpareils. The color of the other nonpareils will get lost in the rainbow sprinkles, and will also make the rainbow sprinkles look off and unbalanced. If you choose to use rainbow nonpareils, decorate with jimmies or mini pearls.

2. Try to mix and match different shapes of sprinkles. For example, use jimmies with nonpareils or mini pearls with nonpareils.

3. Don't shake a sprinkles container over cupcakes. To achieve an even sprinkles look, pour some sprinkles into your palm and then sprinkle with your fingertips over the cupcakes like you're sprinkling salt over food.

4. When you're mixing different shapes of sprinkles, always sprinkle the larger or more bulky ones on first. If you're using jimmies and nonpareils, the jimmies should go first. If you're using mini pearls and nonpareils, the mini pearls should go on first.

5. Don't use jimmies and mini pearls together – it looks too crowded.

6. Never use the same colored but different shaped sprinkles on the same cupcakes.

7. If you only buy one type of sprinkles, buy rainbow nonpareils. They are the most versatile and appropriate for so many occasions.

SPRINKLE INSPIRATIONS

These are some of my go-to sprinkle combinations. Make them your own with whatever colors and combinations suit you.

Rainbow nonpareils
with pink jimmies

Light pink nonpareils
with light blue jimmies

Purple mini pearls
with white nonpareils

Pale green nonpareils
with light pink jimmies

To achieve this swirled look, fill two separate piping bags with the different colors, make a cut about a half inch from the tip, place the two bags in another piping bag and set up with a coupler and a tip, then pipe away!

SHOWSTOPPERS

I love getting creative and trying new decorating techniques.

CROWDPLEASERS

For birthdays, showers and other gatherings, I like to combine decorations to create a bright, happy look.

HANUKKAH HIGHLIGHTS

For holidays I like to experiment with different decorations and methods of frosting.

CHRISTMAS CREATIONS

Creative sprinkles and decorations can be found online from brands like The Layer Cake Shop.

PARTYMAKERS

I get a lot of ideas from Pinterest, and I like to make them my own for parties and celebrations.

LET'S CONNECT

@livsweetcookbook
@olivialuv.bakeshop

olivialuv.bakes

Olivia Luv Bake Shop

Olivia Luv Productions
New York, NY

Made in the USA
Middletown, DE
01 December 2020